T.R.U.S.T
The Reason U See Things

T.R.U.S.T
The Reason U See Things

HE CAN BE.

LORENZO LEE

PALMETTO
P U B L I S H I N G
Charleston, SC
www.PalmettoPublishing.com

Copyright © 2023 by Lorenzo Lee

All rights reserved.

No portion of this book may be reproduced, stored in a retrieval system, or transmitted in any form by any means–electronic, mechanical, photocopy, recording, or other–except for brief quotations in printed reviews, without prior permission of the author.

Paperback ISBN: 979-8-8229-1802-3

ACKNOWLEDGE
...09-10-11-12-14.....

Never Should you forget!

From experiences and encounters with individuals from these times of influence, you manage to obtain the insight to UNDERSTAND in depth why we so called "see". We were taught to believe and achieve happiness from 09-14. I came to the discovery that happiness has become distorted. And what we believe in are reporters not necessarily the report.

You may not want or might not even like it, What Chu need? No. The question is what or whether you believe that you deserve to achieve... Please don't be deceived.

THANK YOU

There are many times thank-you is said throughout the day, every day. But for what and to whom? To whom the thank-you is given to, the person hearing these special words know what it's for. Hopefully you receive a thank you for what is deemed thankful and what seems good to you. And when you do hear it, reply humbly "no problem that's just my style of life."

Any Day It Can Happen

Remove the butterflies from your stomach
Say it can be accomplished
Big trees can be chopped with the right tools and plot
Decide your angle and take a chance
Don't forget to say timber
Remember
Its just like practice a deep breath training exercise
To relieve the stress
What's really on your chest
Pay attention to how they perform when they under duress

Don't estimate any situation. Put your information into an equation and see what the outcome is. This is the best way to determine. Add it up if one and one equals... believe it. You should never try to change the inevitable...

1 on 3. Two on my right. One on the left of Me. The odds are stacked against me but I'm seeing red. I want all of them to bleed. One thing I'm no stranger to risking it... If I fail, at least I was not afraid of the odds to win at all costs.

MAKE UP

We do it to make it look beautiful to the eyes
Studying a thesaurus only for ways to describe
Bolster my vocab hoping I sound better
Hurting them perfect with each letter; give me some sugar
The sweet taste is preferred to my tongue
Is it all worth the chase
We were told to get it until its gone
We all want to be clever
Knowing is often a disadvantage
Those who grow too fast
Grow up to no good.
Whoop they ass while you can
But I aint no judge
The One time I chose to judge and had hate
Fell right on my face and had to change my ways
Now only I choose love the greater of the mind state
I can't let lust get the best of me
All I know is that it takes a perfect recipe
Putting in work that proves your faith
Instead of sitting back waitin
Be able to endure the pain

Hard to Say Nothing

Do what you love and Love what you do
No mater what anyone says
You care so its cool
Who cares if they don't because
This world is huge
If they don't accept your stroke
Go swim in another pool
There will always be sharks so
Be careful to keep your head a float
Now it's at full capacity on this boat
Be aware of the folks you let slide
Not all fights are with guns and knives
Know that knowledge is true power
So if we find what we seek
That's the greatest achievement
That's the only reason we grind hopefully we don't fail in vain
Let success be on the other side
And expect Joy to be on the other side of the pain

Talking Tough, Talkin Drunk

How often I'm at the bank you may assume I'm the banker
You already hear my words slurring so you know I'm a drinker
And I've been drinking so much that my vision getting blurry
And I'm far from home, hoping I get there in a hurry
I got my keys and if I drive the liquor has me un worried
Been through a concussion and totaled a vehicle
Feeling like I should've been buried
Let's keep it real all the time if you will
They say the truth hurts, now that just depends
On how you feel, you can heal from the cuts
When you're certain that's the only blessing
That's the least amount of your stressing
When your words are sincere and you're all about action
You can make it happen and that's no cappin
My babe said she need a little direction
I told her girl I got your back and I'll be your captain

Delusional

I am here, far as hell as I can tell
What the hell is happening here
The world living without any care
They all said fuck it, no fear
Damn right "we'll take it there
If its called for but this is simple
No words that you can get
The same feeling in your mental
I live by own right and that's real
So why try to choose whats right for my life
Do what you do but decide
Does it improve you for the time
Or what moves does it do for life
In general I can be free
Far from the pain if I believe,
What do I want? Is it in reach?
And better is it for me or against?
We make excuses and say GOD
You would provide if it were meant
I'm patient in the same sense
Cuz' it aint what you knew,
It ultimately comes down to what ultimately is true

Foundation

Appreciation delegated to those you want love to be shown
Pardon me for what I know
I don't blame you for nothing you chose, its up to you
Thought you heard the world is yours
I'm sick of hearing of bad news
Not like none of my dues 7 days and can't take a cruise
Say it " fuck the blues" in due time
I'll be up or down
Just remain focus on mind
I'm on my own only here for the dirty work
I hope I clean one day, sometimes life hurts
That builds us to be stronger than the future pain
Its more than what appears to the eyes deep down inside
Is what really counts in due time
Me I'd rather shine in the mirror
You can keep the praise because
We pray its more than just a phase because
Forever we want love to eliminate all forms of hate
The stakes get higher as we climb
There's more to lose than your faith

Growth

The past is important
Really it determines your present
Those negative recollections are the ways I learned my lessons
I can get upset with my friends
I fell in love with my enemies
The struggle is all in my head
Killing myself gradually, addicted to complaining
Thinking my life has me bound and on the ground I will remain
Scared to make a sound
Looking for way up instead constantly going down
Remove the envy from my brain and
I can put together sounds
Like you been talking to me when you said
I hope you never see and as far as success
I'm hoping you never achieve
Who was that speaking to me? Was it me?
I can't be stopped that's what I should say
That should've, could've, would've phrase is so true
Who would've known that opportunity will always be here
It'll last longer than you, so make a move while you can

Glad you Came, stay for a while

The only thing I need is peace
Well a piece of that pumpkin pie
Will you give it to me?
What If I asked nice, use my manners say please
Really just need a slice
The sweet taste on my tongue
Enjoying the pleasures of life
Only comes once, so takes this chance
I'm better than a lifetime
I'll be your favorite program
I'm definitely a pro man with a master plan
Let me master that....
Excuse my language I just want to get my point through
What's your point of view
Don't trip just take a sit back
Lift up your legs and let me kiss that
Its better than French dressing
Only want is for you to know
That you're a huge blessing

Show Me The Way

Re-think, re-plan, all that remember?
Now I'm rewinding, constantly playing the same song
Same track, its ubiquitous,
Everywhere I'm wondering,
If they want us to break our principles
They say its ok for a woman to be president
Whether if you're a man or woman
Gay or straight its irrelevant
We're about to be at a point where nothing even matters
No value, no worth, no facts
Now we want to manipulate the past since when
And its been like that
So we wont stop until we have
But what is gone is left
So they'll create a way to recreate the future
The present doesn't stand a chance

In All Due Reality

Everybody's wish, life minus perils
I wonder if that really exist. Utopia
I wonder if its real can we achieve eternal bliss
I think so, so I begin to drink slow
And to think quick and
I told myself to take my time because
Whatever you want you can get
I speak life into my mind
When everyone else speaks of fear
What's the reason we scream "kill!"
When one comes to challenge the real
What's real to you if its in your tongue
Swallow the truth and taste if it's bitter
Startling revelations all on twitter
One things for sure I'm still a go getter
Public enemy number 1 since the beginning
And I still look inside myself and feel I'm winning
Started looking at my sin record and
Asking God to forgive it and realized
That if I forgive those I'm acquitted.

No patience

It's the either the meaning of respect has changed
Or we're scared to fight
In these times of disagreement no fist
We grab a .9, .32, or .45.
Shoot first and ask questions later
Did he deserve to die?
What happened to win some and lose some in life
If you can deal with the light you'll be alright
It gets bright, you might struggle to see but that's better to me
Than proving your weak
So scared its like a warzone in the streets
You hear "let me get my heat"
We sound tough screaming "ima make that motherfucker bleed"
Somebody has to die. These thoughts derive from greed
I don't want to share this with you
This world ain't enough for me
I'm sick of the shit like my Pop say
That's what a man thinks
If you don't want to get beat to death
Keep your teeth brushed, mouth clean

Letter to THE LORD

Dear God,
Was told that I cannot be here without a purpose
And I thank You for waking me
Making me feel as if I'm worth it
Cuz when I was sleep I had a dream I was worthless
Life unglorified, putting in 15 hours working
Hard labor everyday, trying to earn papers to be free
Guess again freedom belongs to God
We want it to though and to control of the odds
Life and death been in the same state of mind
Wanting to go back in time to rearrange the past
To benefit me forever. Just enjoy that your fam is glad
I'm happy when I can change an attitude
Went from feeling fine in solitude
To your presence giving me gratitude
Cant even be mad at you God
I know all You do is You
Feeling at times your love is not with Me LORD
Or is that my hearting beating selfish
Wanting it all, plus perfection I can't help not wanting flaws
Only thing I ask is prepare for me the falls
Like Jesus Christ said every man
Must bear his own Cross!

Bright side is the Right side

I got less to complain about
Only hearing thank you coming out my mouth
Doubting has never ever been my style
Hoping I'm here for a while
I enjoy the sun, or if there are clouds in the sky
Whether or not the weather is perfect
And despite the folks that hurt you
Pain last but for a moment
A negative emotion is worse than a feeling of burning
My mind is an open wound continually bleeding
In need of a mental bandage
This life I do love it and times I can't stand it
Overall I've accepted and won't take for granted
But I gotta give it back, that's a fact
Check the stats
They'll tell the story of what you lack
Hopefully it aint focus easy to distract

Different Lenses

Robots: Humans perfected,
The real society is neglected
White boys get a pill
Black boys throw em' in a cell
Everyone else will kill each other in a field
Now the only ones who can live here
Are the folks that bow down and keep there lips sealed
Open your mouth and it will be filled.
With a barrel and you will be killed.
Say its all about the dollar bill,
Buy or die.
The only option is to be controlled
What's life without a soul?
This feels like life, without freedom of choice
The only option is to Opt-in or get deployed
I thought if you make your own way
You should receive a reward
I guess the course is a one way tour
I pray for less
More belongs to the Lord

Cherish the Motion

One time for that one time!
Conversations seem different but it's still certain
Keep coastin, and drinks keep em toastin
Party like we'll be here forever
Party like we had it never
Blunts roastin, smell the aroma.
Get off ya ass instead of loafin
In my mind we only have time
Depending on who you are its all fine
Depending on what you can take
It'll be okay.
Ashes to Ashes clay back to clay
Breathe life and watch the form change
You want it all and it won't take a day
Respect is earned not something we take
A starts a start
Even if its just the leaves you rake
Only thing that's at stake
Is what you decide holds weight
Keep your pride don't let anyone take that away
A smile is precious
A smile helps deal with pain

Perseverance is Key

Look at me leap.
I fall every time I attempt to climb
Still won't be discouraged, never giving up
As long as I'm here
No fear even until the day I die
Although I don't know what goes on then
An out of control mind
The only fear is life without a friend
Not really, so I guess I'm always fine
Around those who act like they care
We really don't
We play according to what we deem as fair
As long as I can reach upward
Why would I dare to pursue any other direction
The right way doesn't always seem clear
This life of mine
Ups and downs
It aint fair to who?
To you or me?
Depending the on scene
Only thing I know serene is true peace
Pray on my knees daily
Hoping I stay stable and able to
To keep my sanity
This world will try to change you

Absolute Value

All my life I wanted Joy
So I bought it
Fought for it
Worked for it even
Stole for it
Till I prayed for it
Remained for it
Gotta grow up one day
The world I'm enjoyin it
Women and wine
Liquor and trees
A hell of a time
The only concern of me,
Can't figure it out
Why continually scream
When its all about how to smile
Sacrifices are a part of life
Have it all and control
Aware of the direction
The greatest knowledge of life
Which way to go to become who you are
You'll say "way to go
I'm feelin like gold"
Hold on and cherish the moments
That give fulfillment to your soul

Ready or Not

Down mentally I can't think,
Damn I can't see
Damn I can't put together me,
Damn I can't reach
I'm out of range in a strange place
Damn I can't change position
Damn I'm out of shape
In search for the one at fault
Can't even find a mirror
Damn I'm fuckin lost
Damn I'm the one to blame
Damn I done lost touch and
It's a damn shame
Damn am I insane
Who ask that question? Was it me
Had to be
I'm half alone, half depressed, half deceased
In way over my head but
Damn I'm damned
Get it together because
I am the man

Perfect Situation

Why is it that
We should look a certain way
Act a certain way
Display certain things
Conceal certain things
Reveal certain things
Certainly it's a strain
Everyday is a performance
The audience will slay
Hands down if they don't approve
Approve in what you believe
Certainly I been dealt with crude
Certainly I been played
Feelin at times I've been the fool
We all have to be
So I guess I should keep it cool
Content with the fuckery
That surrounds me daily
Basically just maintaining
Steadily thinking like,
Hell the world is always changing
One thing is for certain
We have to be courageous
At all times I'm just sayin

Mention Me When You Pray

Stronger than ever forever
Realized I have to go
Everything must change
New becomes old
Birth to decay
Also Darkness will bring light
And back dark again
Black forever say,
Black as the universe in the sky constantly
But they say blacks are beast
They got it confused with what lies underneath
We all have the need to survive
Black forever resides
Just close your eyes
Death in disguise
Many times I've attempted
Also many times I didn't
Where do we finish
Went to hell and back
Start from the beginning
Tryin to get back to Heaven

Ps and Qs

Running out of words to say
I might just leave a blank page
And know that things change
Always coming to a different age
Five to ten, to fifteen, to twenty-five
Only thing I can say
Is I'm glad I'm still alive
I say thank God for breath
I felt like I heard God just say
Don't thank me just yet
By the times its all said and done
You will be prayin for death
Let the Earth fall on me
And remember me less
God why I ask You appear
If I would've known
That my soul you would pierce
Instead of just sayin that I care
I might cut my hair
And be aware of what I say
And aware of how I hear
In life what's really the situation
Its always fucked up prior to feeling amazing

Take a Second Look

Vow to me,
You wont say WOW
When you see how I shine
If it was to me
I'd rather stay out of sight
Know when you look in the constantly
It'll eventually ruin your eyes
My vision tainted since I was five
Told myself we live for pieces of paper
Age nine, realized I wanted to be a player
Fly whips, a bunch of money
Just a million I wanted
But like I said I had tainted vision
Everything that's incorporated with the picture
The strokes it takes to paint it
Guaranteed that I missed it
Do you get it
It takes more than eyes to guide
Can't forget your hearing
We lose our sense of touch and
Fail to decipher the smell
So we forget to taste it correct
And say please I don't want to go to Hell

No Title Necessary

No name
So I'm here forever
Each road I take
Whatever endeavor I'll make
Create for the better
My destiny is great
Can you relate to the way
Are you aware of the truth
Said it'll set you free
We let the lie intrude
Want to just sip on some tea
While enjoying a cruise
How much work is involved
Which way is right
In a world filled with wrong
Each day is the same
We all do it to be great
I put these words on a page
I may just read them myself
Take this stress of my brain
This is my ideal of help
Call on me if you need
Hopefully you need someone to speak positively
Deep down I need you to believe in you

Mine in due time

My daily chant Lord
Help me if You want to
I definitely know You can
You understand I'm not perfect
I cant speak for every man
The places I've come across
All the folks that I've met
I had some crazy encounters
That's why I'm due my respects
Paid tribute before
Plenty of times took the backseat
Now give him what he's entitled to
Life of luxury
Instead of these hotel rooms
I agree with you too
Life can be sweet
It can be sour too
Especially if you cheat
You tricked me for a second but
I'll get back at you eventually
At a certain turn of events we pray
We change from poor to fortunate

Mindset

Mama whooped my ass
Never said I'm going to get ya Dad
Pop aint give a fuck
When the bottle was in his hand
Still a hell of a soldier
Took care of all 5 of his kids
Never afraid to go and get it
Even if they said it was off limits
Or on top of the mountains
Still we all have doubts
Couldn't keep it together
Just to say we count
Separate endeavors for us all
So we stay afloat never drowning
If we had to we'd build a boat
Theres no such thing as an impossible challenge
Stereotype for balance
Peace on my mind
No matter what you can't take it
Prepare for a fight
Guaranteed I'll keep my head
Forever holdin it high
I thank the Lord for the sky

Instructions

To be a son
You have to more
Listen up and imply
Every strategy know
You won't be denied
Do what you can
Instead of sayin its to much to try
I know its tough losin sleep
Tired and it shows
On the outside that your weak
But underneath remain strong
Whatever they think
Let em think
Right or wrong
The choice is yours to keep your peace

Truth be told

Only you can make me change
Only you can make me say
Only your word will I obey
Only your style I appreciate
Only we could be a team
Only we could do anything
Only I can make you sweat
Only I can take your hand
We used to do it for our mamas
Now we all want to be Obama
What's wrong with the world
We used to want to discover
Reveal a way to help another
Now we just want to destroy
Take control because its never enough
We need the Earth, Moon and stars
Hot like the sun
You heard it before
Its not all about the money
So give it away
Every dollar not saving 1 for enjoyment

All In

They say life's a struggle
I say take your time
Utilize each second
Strategize what happens next
It'll be just fine
Feeling like I went suicide
It must be do or die
If there's a cause
We gotta do more than just try
The consequence is death
Give all you can to life
It aint about what you can't
Focus on what's at hand
Guarantee to rise to the top
If we fulfill our plan
Truth is in life I fail to understand
On how we live according
To the standards of the next man
And status is it fair?
I guess so it depends on the circumstance
Take a chance on a person
And if they get an F
You pronounce them as dead
Life is just a test

JustBeYou(JBY)

You heard it before
At times you be trippin
I'm here to remind you
Aint nothing wrong with being an individual
Its in the scripture to judge not
You will be picked
With my angels in Heaven
Taking care of all my footsteps
Each step I take
I pray it takes me to you
I never knew you
I must be stupid
My attention span shorter
Than a kindergarten students
For real at time I know I need a tutor
Life worries on my brain
Infect me like a flu or a disease inside
And I don't know what else to do
Say don't worry bout a thing
It'll be all cool says who?

www.ingramcontent.com/pod-product-compliance
Lightning Source LLC
LaVergne TN
LVHW041643070526
838199LV00053B/3525